D1795133

The
Yorkshire Dales

Peter Young

COUNTRYSIDE BOOKS
NEWBURY BERKSHIRE

First published 2008
© Peter Young, 2008

All rights reserved. No reproduction
permitted without the prior permission
of the publisher:

COUNTRYSIDE BOOKS
3 Catherine Road
Newbury, Berkshire

To view our complete range of books,
please visit us at
www.countrysidebooks.co.uk

ISBN 978 1 84674 086 2

For Janet

Photographs by the author
Maps by CJWT Solutions

Designed by Peter Davies, Nautilus Design

Produced through MRM Associates Ltd, Reading
Typeset by CJWT Solutions, St Helens
Printed by Information Press, Oxford

*All material for the manufacture of this book
was sourced from sustainable forests*

Contents

Location Map   4

Introduction   5

POCKET PUB WALKS

1. Austwick *(4 miles)*   7
2. Chapel-le-Dale *(2½ or 5½ miles)*   12
3. Dent *(4 miles)*   17
4. Sedbergh *(3¼ miles)*   22
5. Hardraw *(4 miles)*   27
6. Muker *(4¾ miles)*   31
7. Langthwaite *(4, 3 or 2½ miles)*   36
8. Redmire *(5 miles)*   41
9. Carlton-in-Coverdale *(6¼ miles)*   46
10. Bishopdale *(4 miles)*   51
11. Hubberholme *(3 miles)*   56
12. Hebden *(6¼ or 3 miles)*   61
13. Embsay *(3½ miles)*   66
14. Kirkby Malham *(6¼ or 2½ miles)*   71
15. Helwith Bridge *(4½ miles)*   76

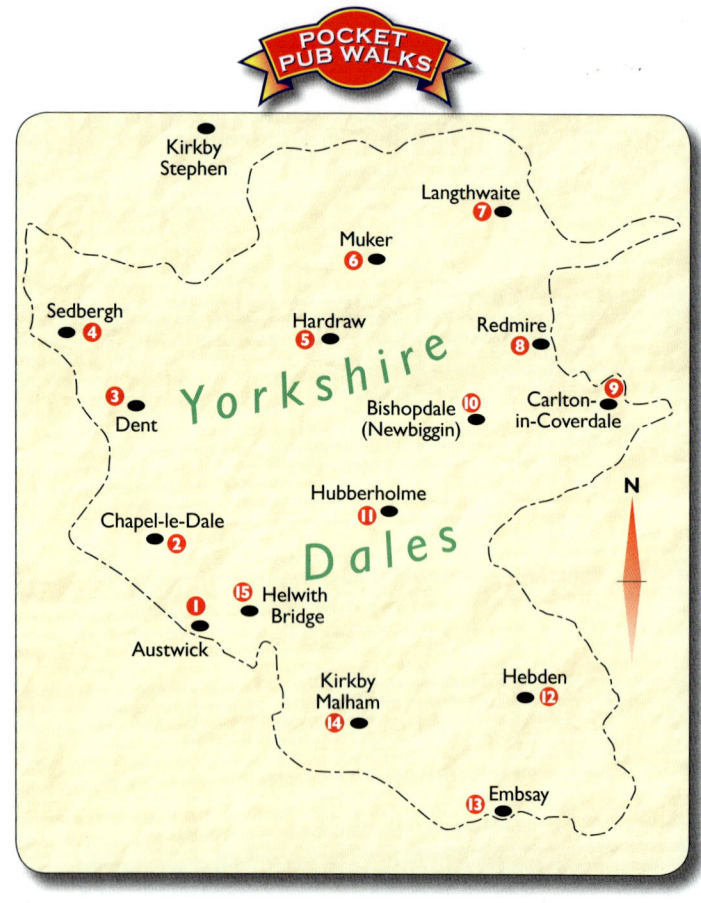

POCKET
PUB WALKS

Kirkby
Stephen

Langthwaite
7

Muker
6

Sedbergh
4

Hardraw
5

Redmire
8

Yorkshire

3

Dent

Bishopdale
(Newbiggin)
10

Carlton-
in-Coverdale
9

Hubberholme
11

N

Chapel-le-Dale
2

Dales

15 Helwith
Bridge

1

Austwick

Kirkby
Malham
14

Hebden
12

Embsay
13

Area map showing location of the walks

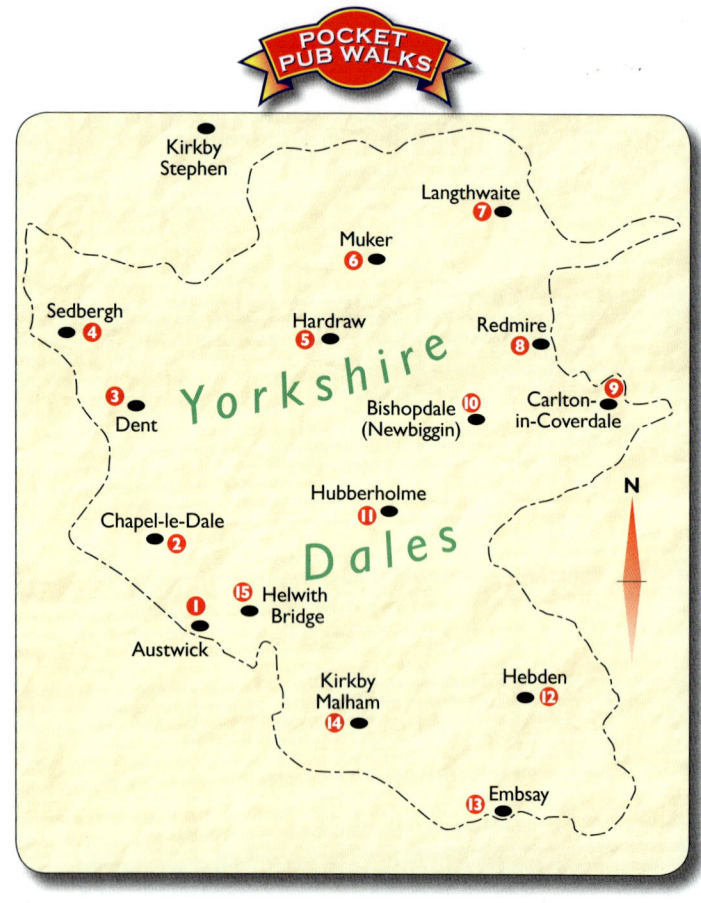

Introduction

The prospect of a day out in the Yorkshire Dales is something most people look forward to. This area of fine landscapes has always been a magnet for visitors, who appreciate the Dales scenery – the blend of green valleys and high hills, the random patterns of drystone walls and attractive, stone-built villages.

The walks described in this book each start and finish at a Dales pub. The public houses featured here pride themselves on their food, drink and hospitality. Most have been a focal point in their locality for years. The phrase 'the Pub is the Hub' was first used in 2001 by the Prince of Wales. His support for village inns led to an initiative which has benefited rural communities and businesses in many areas, including the Dales.

Though there are plenty of modern aspects of life in the Dales to appreciate, anyone who walks here becomes conscious of the past. History is all around in the characteristic place-names, the old buildings and ancient churches, abbeys and castles as well as the former industrial buildings such as mills and mines.

Hopefully the sketch maps will help you to follow the route, but the best map is the Ordnance Survey. You don't need many of these for the walks in this book as the relevant sheets are two-sided and cover a large area. The great detail our fine OS maps contain adds interest to any visit.

In hilly places like the Dales the weather can change quickly and paths may be slippery in any weather so wear appropriate footwear and have spare clothing and waterproofs. Please check before you park at the pub, in several places adequate parking is available nearby but, if not, respect the needs of local people.

Let's hope you have good weather to enjoy the Yorkshire Dales – the spectacular views, heather moorlands, sparkling rivers, the pubs – and all best seen on foot!

Peter Young

Publisher's Note

We hope that you obtain considerable enjoyment from this book; great care has been taken in its preparation. However, changes of landlord and actual closures are sadly not uncommon. Likewise, although at the time of publication all routes followed public rights of way or permitted paths, diversion orders can be made and permissions withdrawn.

We cannot, of course, be held responsible for such diversion orders and any inaccuracies in the text which result from these or any other changes to the routes nor any damage which might result from walkers trespassing on private property. We are anxious though that all details covering the walks are kept up to date and would therefore welcome information from readers which would be relevant to future editions.

The simple sketch maps that accompany the walks in this book are based on notes made by the author whilst checking out the routes on the ground. However, for the benefit of a proper map, we do recommend that you purchase the relevant Ordnance Survey sheet covering your walk. The Ordnance Survey maps are widely available, especially through booksellers and local newsagents.

1 Austwick

The Game Cock Inn

I t is well worth a diversion off the busy A65 to visit the pleasant village of Austwick and to find peace and quiet. All around the valley are rocky outcrops which seem to burst out of the green hillsides. Sometimes from a distance you may not be sure whether you see sheep or a rock. Though the narrow lanes may not be driver-friendly the paths are welcoming. On the way round this route you cross two becks by some clapper bridges, using stone slabs which are an unusual feature. At the second bridge an old sheep wash is an ideal picnic spot, before you walk through a fine Dales landscape back to Austwick. On the Spring Bank Holiday Monday there is usually a Cuckoo Festival held in the village which commemorates an event of long ago. I leave that to you!

The Yorkshire Dales

Distance – 4 miles.

OS Explorer Outdoor Leisure OL2, Yorkshire Dales, Southern & Western areas. GR 767685.

Starting point The Game Cock Inn bordering the village green in Austwick.

How to get there Austwick lies one mile off the A65 between Settle and Clapham. There are three turnings from the main road. From the south turn right about five miles after the start of the Settle by-pass, look out for the turn to Feizor, and Austwick is next. From the north take a left turn about one mile from Clapham. Consider the residents when parking in the village.

THE PUB The **Game Cock Inn** has twice won the Thwaites' Brewery accolade of 'Catering Pub of the Year'. Its facilities and service include a French accent to the large menu, such as the boeuf bourguignon, a traditional French dish. The Game Cock Pie has venison, rabbit and game birds. Apart from the regular, Thwaites, there are guest beers. The winter months in these parts can be chilly so the Game Cock has open fires to keep visitors snug. Comfortable B&B accommodation is available.

Food is served from 11.30 am to 2 pm every day and all day Sundays. Dinner is from 6 pm to 9 pm and booking is advisable.
☎ *01524 251226*

1 From the **Game Cock** turn left on the pavement and walk past interesting cottages and the school. Keep on where the pavement ends and go next right at a bridleway track, signed to **Feizor**. The track you take is part of the **Pennine Bridleway**, a national

trail. Continue to a stream which you can cross by the slabs of **Flascoe Bridge**. There is a seat nearby. Continue a few yards to a wall stile on the left and cross into a large field. The wall on the left is not straight and you pass near a corner of it as you go up over the field, on a path which is only lightly marked. In the top corner there is a stile.

2 Turn left onto an enclosed lane. Ignore a right turn and go round bends then along a straighter section. Keep on the lane passing Wood End Farm and reach a road. Go right a few yards to a bridleway on the left for **Crummack Dale**. There is an old Dales barn on your right. Go up the track to the hamlet of **Wharfe**.

The clapper bridge at Wash Dub Fold

3 Reach a T-junction between two buildings and go over a lane and up slightly left. **Garth Cottage** is on your right as you climb a track away from the houses. This enclosed path is followed for about a mile, there are two barns on your left at first and gradually views of the valley are revealed. The thick hedge has flowers and bird life – wrens are about and we saw a pheasant. The surface is stony at times and when another track joins from a field it becomes wider. Bear left then arrive at the clapper bridge over **Austwick Beck**. This is **Wash Dub Fold** – a lovely spot for a break. There is a second bridge and a seat and a notice board explains the area. Field scabious grows by the stream.

4 Leave by the main bridge and go along the track to a gap on the left, there is a wall stile to cross into a field. Walk away from the stile on a path other people have used, but it is not heavily walked and is very pleasant through this open land, a contrast to the earlier enclosed tracks. Climb gradually and keep to the right of the rocky areas you see to your left. As you breast the hill there is a stile in the wall ahead, by a wooden post.

5 The path continues ahead, this should show on the ground and in the distance your next stiles may be seen. Drop down and cross the large open field, look for a lone tree and to its right there is a barn. Make for the wooden stile to the right of the barn, and from here go slightly right to a wall. Follow this a few yards to a footpath sign at a stile. Do not cross the stile, keep in the field and follow the arrow pointing down the field and signed to **Austwick**.

6 The sloping shape of Pendle Hill can be seen in the distance, in Lancashire, as you head for a small bridge over a stream before a wall stile to the right of a barn. Go ahead by a wall and a stile to enter the yard of **Town Head Farm**. Cross to a second stile where you now cross a garden – do not linger here – to reach a road. Turn left and go down it, you will soon recognise the road from where you set out and a right turn brings you back to the village green in Austwick and the **Game Cock Inn**.

Places of interest nearby

The **Yorkshire Dales Falconry Centre** on the A65, just south of Austwick, has many birds of prey and there are flying displays throughout the year.
☎ *01729 822832.*

At the next village of Clapham a nature trail leads through the picturesque Farrer estate to **Ingleborough Cave**, where you can experience underground tours of this spectacular show cave.
☎ *01524 251242*

2 Chapel-le-Dale

The Old Hill Inn

One of the best known pubs in the Dales, the Old Hill Inn is a favourite starting point for a walk up Ingleborough, 2,373 ft high. However, neither the short or longer walk described here goes to the top, but by setting off in the opposite direction you can have a fine view of Ingleborough instead, and of Whernside. The famous Ribblehead Viaduct can be seen on both walks and the shorter route provides good views of the area without going as far as the viaduct. At the little church in Chapel-le-Dale there is a plaque commemorating over 100 men who died during the construction of the Settle to Carlisle railway. Apart from a longer and a shorter route there are two suggested one-mile extensions – so, plenty of choice!

Distance – 2½ miles or 5½ miles, with optional extensions.

OS Explorer Outdoor Leisure OL2, Yorkshire Dales, Southern & Western areas. GR 743776.

Starting point The Old Hill Inn at Chapel-le-Dale.

How to get there *The Old Hill Inn is on the B6255 between Ingleton, about 4 miles, and Ribblehead, about 2 miles. Parking at the pub is limited but there is a lay-by nearby.*

THE PUB

The **Old Hill Inn** is ancient and parts of it date back to 1615. Even the new bits are of 1835 vintage. It has always been a popular rendezvous for outdoor people. You might meet cavers – there are many caves in the area – or maybe walkers doing the 'Three Peaks'. They could be enjoying a Dent Aviator beer or Theakston's Best Bitter, or drying themselves in front of the log fires. Black Sheep Best and Timothy Taylor's Landlord are also enjoyed in the cosy bar. A family of chefs run the Old Hill Inn and the food is taken seriously here. Rib-eye steak and lamb shank are popular meat dishes and the fish are worth considering. You may be shown the sugar sculpture which has been featured in local publications.

Food is served from 12 noon to 2.30 pm and 6.30 pm to 8.30 pm, 6 pm Saturdays, evening booking is advisable. Closed all day Mondays.
☎ *01524 241256*

1 Cross the road from the **Old Hill Inn** and turn left for 100 yards to a gate and cattle grid on the right. Walk along the lane, known as **Philpin Lane**, passing a house of that name. Continue past a farm and soon the lane bends left.

The Yorkshire Dales

6 Turn left down a track for a fine descent. There are striking views of **Whernside** behind you and **Ingleborough** ahead. After about a mile reach the hamlet of **Chapel-le-Dale**. Some well-known potholes, with evocative names, are over the walls. How did Hurtle Pot and Jingle Pot get their names, for instance? At a junction go left and see **St Leonard's church**. A short distance ahead you can join the road and return, with care on it, to the **Old Hill Inn**.

7 *There is an option of a walk of about one mile from the stile over the road.* You will have extensive views of where you have walked. From the stile go up to another in a second wall. Climb to a wooden stile from where you pass in front of the house at **Souther Scales**. Go through a wall gap to a stile – signed to Ingleborough, but do not go in that direction! Go ahead up the field, bearing left to a second gap, (yellow mark). From a metal gate walk up a fine green path to a ladder stile. The path goes by the wall, then climbs to the right with the wall on the left. Reach a post signed to '**Sleights Road** $3/8$' and follow this, gradually descending across the long field to a new gate in the wall. Take a clear path to the road and the **Old Hill Inn** is to the left.

Place of interest nearby

At **Ribblehead Station**, the visitor centre tells the story of the Settle to Carlisle Railway, including the Ribblehead Viaduct which stands nearby. Open daily 9.30 am to 4 pm except Monday from Easter to October. Except Monday and Tuesday late October and November.

White Scar Cave 3 miles south is the longest show cave in Britain with an 80-minute guided tour. Open daily February to October, weekends November to January. ☎ *01524 241244.*

3 **Dent**

The Sun Inn

he seclusion of Dentdale is one reason why it is a favourite area for many lovers of the Dales. Access to the valley is not easy by road, but the cobbled streets and whitewashed cottages of Dent are a great attraction. Dent station, at 1,132 ft above sea level the highest main-line station in England, is four miles from the village, and interesting to visit. This walk uses some of the pleasant footpaths from the village and provides views of the green valley which will stay in the memory. From Tommy Bridge you see the valley of Deepdale and the walk along the Dales Way by the River Dee back to Dent is always a treat.

The Yorkshire Dales

Distance – 4 miles.

OS Explorer Outdoor Leisure OL2, Yorkshire Dales, Southern & Western areas. GR 705870.

Starting point The Sun Inn at Dent.

How to get there Dent is reached off the A683 near Sedbergh. In Barbon village look for the signs to Dent. From the B6255 Ingleton to Hawes road, turn west 5 miles north of Ribblehead. There is a village car park.

THE PUB

'The Best Ales & Food under the Sun' proclaims the sign outside the **Sun Inn**. After sampling its hospitality you will probably agree, the no-nonsense bar food includes home-made soup, a big basket of chips, and beef or cheeseburgers. On the blackboard for the 'Meat Eaters' Specials of the Day', I noticed sausage cassoulet which sounded interesting. Children have their own menu and curry is popular with the clientele who include campers and caravanners. They are well catered for with an intriguing choice of real ales. Try the local Dent Brewery's Kamikaze or maybe Oakham Brewery's Bishop's Farewell. A real fire will welcome you if the weather is cool. The Sun also offers accommodation.

Food is served from 12 noon to 2 pm and 6.30 pm to 8.30 pm.
☎ *01539 625208*

1 From the **Sun Inn** go down the main cobbled street which becomes a road as you leave the village. Go on and cross **Church Bridge** over the **River Dee**. Keep on the road as it bears right and after about 250 yards and an old milepost, turn up a track

on the left. The outer sides are concreted, and you reach a farm, **Hall Bank**. Go to the right in front of the cottages and through a small yard. Look for a stile on the right into a field and from here the direction is straight ahead for about a mile. Walk by the wall to a stile at the end. Turn left on a track and continue in front of the houses and barn. Go into a field to a gate and cross a field. Go through a metal gate and turn right on an enclosed track. Walk in front of a house and turn left through a pair of wooden gates. Go right by the **Hayloft** and over a small footbridge crossing **Backstone Gill**.

2 Continue on a track enclosed by a hedge and wall. From a gate go right then left on a metalled track. Turn left at a sign up into a field and turn right by a wall, above a property. Go through the stile in the wall ahead and look for the yellow marker ahead, at a squeeze stile in a wall. Turn left to enter a wooded area. There is a slab bridge over **Scotcher Gill**. Cross a farm track to a stile and go over a field. From a wall stile go to a wooden stile

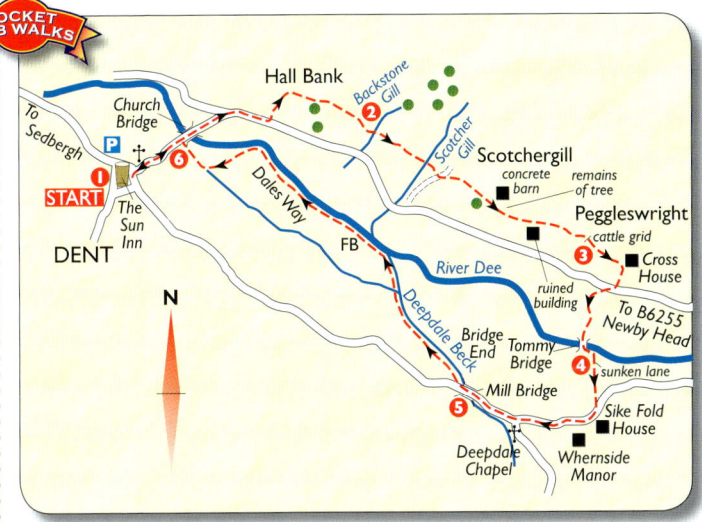

The Yorkshire Dales

The River Dee

at a slightly lower level by the remains of a large tree. Cross a field in front of a concrete barn to a large wooden step stile in the corner. Go along the field to the left of a property, note arrow. Reach a wall and a very narrow squeeze above a ruined building. Continue through a field to a stile in the next wall. Go up slightly over a field to a wooden stile. From here join a track serving the property to the left, **Pegglewright**, a house with a white front facing a long barn.

3 There is a cattle grid immediately left, but turn right and walk down the track. Keep on this main track and pass **Cross House** as you go down. Reach the valley road. Cross slightly right and into the farmyard, the signpost reads **Cross House Lane**. Go through the gate on the left and down to a second gate, do not go through. Follow the sign to **Tommy Bridge**, going down the field with the hedge on your left. The land is often wet. When you reach a gate accessing an enclosed track continue ahead to **Tommy Bridge**, spanning the **River Dee**.

4 Turn left a few yards to a narrow sunken lane and follow this to reach a quiet road. Turn right and go along at first passing **Syke Fold** then you see **Whernside Manor**, a Grade II listed building. Next you reach **Deepdale Chapel** where there are a few gravestones. Over the wall there is a fine view down to **Deepdale Beck**. Go on a little and the road crosses **Mill Bridge**.

5 Look on the right for the signpost pointing to **Church Bridge** and follow the **Dales Way** route for 1½ miles to **Dent**. At first you are beside **Deepdale Beck** until the **River Dee** joins. As you go along the riverside path you see Dent coming into view. Reach a wide flat crossing from where you go beside the football field to a black kissing gate.

6 Turn left on the road into **Dent**. Take the gate on the right through the churchyard, there is a war memorial with a moving tribute and the church may be open. Continue on the path and go left for the **Sun Inn**. Nearby the granite memorial commemorates **Adam Sedgwick**, a local boy who became Woodwardian Professor of Geology at Cambridge University. His pupils included the young Charles Darwin.

Places of interest nearby

Dent Village Heritage Centre has an interesting display on the lives of local people through the centuries and many aspects of farming, wildlife and local culture.
☎ *01539 625800*
Flintergill Outrake Nature Trail is a short linear walk to a fine viewpoint which starts in the centre of Dent. You can see the 'Dancing Flags' which are explained in a leaflet from the Heritage Centre.

4 Sedbergh

The Dalesman Country Inn

For a small town, Sedbergh has a lot going for it. Situated in the north-west corner of the National Park, it has its own distinctive identity and has achieved the status of a 'Book Town'. With many book shops and a famous public school, it's a pleasant place to live, as we were told by people we met there. No doubt local people are proud that the Quaker movement had its origins in the area. Behind Sedbergh stand the Howgills, open hills giving wonderful views which you walk on the way to a local viewpoint called Winder. Though it is only in the foothills of the Howgills, this walk climbs 1,200 feet and is the steepest ascent in this book. I hope this will not put you off because you walk on fine springy ground for the most part and the descent is interesting.

Distance – 3¼ miles.

OS Explorer Outdoor Leisure OL19, Howgill Fells & Upper Eden Valley. There are local footpath maps available. GR 657921.

Starting point The Dalesman Country Inn on Main Street.

How to get there *Sedbergh stands at the crossroads of the A683 between Kirkby Lonsdale and Kirkby Stephen and the A684 between Kendal and Wensleydale. From the M6 motorway follow the A684 from junction 37. There are several car parks including at the east end of Main Street, near the Tourist office.*

THE PUB When we called at the **Dalesman Country Inn** there was a convivial atmosphere and we were soon being given suggestions for suitable walks in the neighbourhood. Everyone seemed to be an ambassador for the pub, and the town, and keen to sing their praises. The Dalesman is nicely situated in the town centre and it's a spacious building. The beers available include Tetley's and Guinness, as well as Dalesman Bitter. Tuesdays are Pie Nights and it's Jazz Night on the first Monday in the month. The menu includes about 20 main courses, such as Tiger prawn salad and Hereford beef sirloin. The specials board is often updated and on the lunch menu is a Full Monty breakfast. There are choices for children.

Food is served all day Saturday and Sunday, Monday to Friday lunch from 12 noon to 2 pm and dinner from 6 pm to 9 pm.
☎ *01539 621183*

The Yorkshire Dales

1 From the **Dalesman Inn** turn right on the pavement and immediately after the building go right up the lane. Continue straight up, over the crossroads, and pass between the end of **Fairholme** on the right and the **People's Hall** and football field on your left. Keep on the lane, past Havera, and turn right at the signed 'Permissive path to the fell'. Reach **Lockbank Farm** and go slightly right through the yard and up a bridleway. At the end reach open land and there is a seat nearby to enjoy the view.

2 Turn left from the gate and follow a path by the wall. The area is well walked and there are several major and minor paths

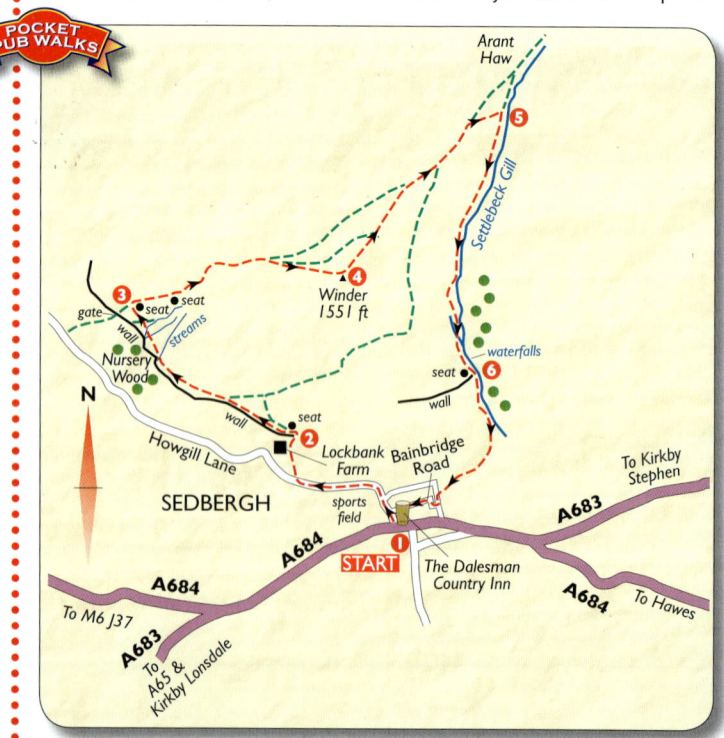

Sedbergh (Walk 4

Arant Haw seen from Winder

about. At first ignore a path sloping up to the right. Look for a wooded area called **Nursery Wood** over the wall. Streams running down may require care to cross. Go on a little further to a seat commanding a widespread view, with railway viaducts and the M6 motorway to the west. Trains on the West Coast main line can be seen as you go on the steady climb to Winder's summit.

3. The gate below is an access point for walkers. A path continues up from the gate and passes a few yards to the left of a seat. Join it along a slightly sunken path, leading up to a wider path which reaches a plateau where there is another seat, to the right. Continue up on a wide path between bracken. This pleasant path continues steadily upwards to the top of **Winder**. There is an Ordnance Survey trig point and a viewfinder. This was erected for the Millennium and you can identify the features of the widespread scene.

4 Check the direction to **Arant Haw**, towards which the route continues at first, and notice the paths ahead going off to the right. The walking on a clear and wide track is a taste of the Howgills, it is unfenced and open land. Unless you fancy going on to Arant Haw, take the second path right, a short cut going diagonally which joins a track coming down.

5 Turn right and go down beside the ravine gouged out by **Settlebeck Gill**. From here Winder already looks to be very high and far off. This south facing descent is a fine experience, with the **Rawthey valley** below but the path requires care. You need to leave the Gill before a ledge and cross to the right over a minor stream to join a good path. At a fork go left down a rocky section. The stream flows down a wide and stony bed and your objective is a kissing gate where a wall ahead reaches close to the stream. When you get down, a seat and a bench near the gate are definitely worth a stop.

6 From the kissing gate access the strip of green land between the trees and fence. The green gives way to a metalled track, then a road as you get towards the town and you reach **Joss Lane** in **Sedbergh**. Continue down here to **Bainbridge Road** and go right along it. Look out for an urban footpath on the left. Go down this a few yards and bear right to reach almost the front door of the **Dalesman**.

Place of interest nearby

The **Brigflatts Quaker Meeting** is west of the town. Dating from 1675, this is the oldest Meeting House in the north of England, and visitors come to experience the peaceful and welcoming atmosphere.
☎ *015396 20005.*

5 **Hardraw**

The Green Dragon Inn

To see Hardraw Force, England's highest unbroken **waterfall**, you go through the Green Dragon Inn. There is a charge to walk through a large natural amphitheatre, where brass bands sometimes perform, to admire the 100 ft cascade. Not only does the pub own Hardraw Force; the Green Dragon is also on the route of the Pennine Way, so the walk starts and finishes on it. You see Appersett Viaduct over which trains once ran, pass through the market town of Hawes and enjoy a stroll beside the meandering River Ure.

THE PUB **The Green Dragon Inn** is a legendary free house. Its innkeeper is the self-styled 'Waterfall Provider' and beer aficionados will find themselves well provided for too, with a wide choice, including real ales from Theakston's and Black Sheep Brewery. You can try Timothy Taylor's Landlord, as well as sampling lesser-known local beers. The pub's home-made

Distance – 4 miles.

OS Explorer Outdoor Leisure OL30, Yorkshire Dales, Northern & Central areas. GR 867913.

Starting point The Green Dragon Inn at Hardraw.

How to get there Hardraw lies one mile north of Hawes and roads run there from each end of the town. Parking is available nearby on the lane.

steak pie, the curries and the fish dishes are popular and it is worth checking the 'Specials' board before you decide. 'Light Bites' are available at the bar. Baguettes and sandwiches are available and children have their own menu. Look out for live music events at weekends. The inn also offers accommodation.

The pub is open all day, every day.
☎ *01969 667392*

1 With a right turn from the **Green Dragon**, cross the bridge over **Hardraw Beck**. Pass the houses and the outdoor centre and go right on the first lane, signed for the **Pennine Way** to **Thwaite**, and other places. Follow this wide track for about ¾ mile. As you climb, fine views emerge of this remote countryside. Pass a plantation on the left and reach a signpost at a gate pointing to **New Bridge**. Leave the **Pennine Way** and descend slightly left on a grassy path over rough land, named as Bluebell Hill on the OS map. Cross a stile in the wall below and from a signpost the way is marked by posts across a hillside to a wooden gate in a wall. Drop down to the gate you see below, there is a slab footbridge just before it. Go ahead over the field to a stile by the road, the A684.

2 Take the **Hawes road** and go over the 'weak bridge' – break step as you go. This is really **New Bridge** and immediately after the parapet on the right climb down a ladder to a footpath. Go left parallel with the road, rejoining it at the farm entrance. Cross the bridge over **Widdale Beck** into **Appersett**. Turn right on the road by the beck. Soon reach the impressive **Appersett Viaduct** which has remained in situ since the Wensleydale Railway closed in 1964.

3 Take the footpath on the left after the viaduct. Cross diagonally to a stile in the wall above. The path is not heavily walked and at least one waymark was knocked over when I was prospecting

the route. The path is better up to a metal gate in a higher wall. Continue diagonally over the next field to an old house, **Spillian Green** on the OS map. Nearby go through the stile in the wall next to a tree. There is another wall stile ahead, and further on a slab footbridge. After one more stile go through a big metal gate in a series of fences, with buildings on the right. Go ahead on a track and reach a road.

4 Turn right and shortly walk into **Hawes**. Go along the main street and you may want to look around the town. *To continue the route:* From the **Market Place**, opposite the chippie, go on a short lane to the right of **Littlefairs** ironmongery shop. See the public footpath sign on the wall. Turn left before the yard in front of the houses to a small gate. Cross the field and go through a gate and right across two fields. Walk under the railway line and down to the **River Ure**. Turn right over a stile for the start of a riverside section. There are metal ladder-stiles and steps and you can enjoy the **Ure** as it twists and turns. Because the river bends back on itself the path turns sharp right from a ladder stile. Cross a footbridge over **Gayle Beck** and reach the road at **Haylands Bridge**.

5 Turn left over the bridge and go on the road up to the second path, not the first, for **Hardraw**. This is the **Pennine Way** and is easy to follow. At a gap, and where the first **Hardraw** path comes in, there is a well-known flagged section over the fields. Follow this and you reach **Hardraw** in front of the **Green Dragon**.

Place of interest nearby

The Dales Countryside Museum in the Station Yard at Hawes brings alive the story of the people and landscape of the Dales and includes a 'time tunnel'. ☎ *01969 666210*

6 **Muker**

The Farmers Arms

For many people, **Swaledale** is their favourite Yorkshire dale. Its scenery provides the views often featured on postcards, calendars and souvenirs that visitors take home to remind them of visits to the Dales. On this walk you follow the tumbling River Swale to Ivelet Bridge. The return on the opposite side of the valley gives wonderful panoramas of the dale. There is a section which requires some care before reaching Muker. The view of the village with its stone bridge, church and huddle of cottages may be a familiar scene. Another image of Swaledale often portrayed is of the old stone barns standing in fields of yellow buttercups in summer, under a warm sun, with a blue sky and white fleecy clouds.

The Yorkshire Dales

Distance – 4¾ miles.

OS Explorer Outdoor Leisure OL30, Yorkshire Dales, Northern & Central areas. GR 910978.

Starting point The Farmers Arms in Muker.

How to get there *Muker is 10 miles west of Reeth on the B6270 through Swaledale. From Askrigg and Hawes in Wensleydale, moorland roads run north to Swaledale. There is a village car park.*

THE PUB

The **Farmers Arms** stands in the centre of Muker and welcomes walkers with its range of food and drinks. You can sample Black Sheep Best and John Smith's Ales, and the Farmers has Theakston's Old Peculier Best Bitter, with guest ales usually there in summer. There are separate lunch and evening menus, with a specials board which is worth checking. When we were there, Sunday lunch roasts arrived and we saw many happy faces about! Medallions of beef cooked in Guinness looked interesting or you could try the shepherd's pie. You may prefer a jacket potato with a choice of fillings, plus a salad. There is a children's menu.

Food is served from 12 noon to 2.30 pm and 6 pm to 8.45 pm daily.
01748 886297

1 From the **Farmers Arms** turn left and walk up the road into the village, past the No Through Road sign and the **Literary Institute** on your right. On the right of the houses facing you follow the footpath signed to **Gunnerside** and **Keld**. Go through a gap stile by a metal gate and through a field. Soon you are walking on a continuous paved path through fields. Reach a right turn for **Gunnerside** and cross **Ramps Holme Bridge**. The view of the **Swale** is enjoyable in every season, any weather.

2 From the bridge the path going right is less easy to walk on than the approach to the bridge. Reach a stile at a barn and go to the right of a house to a wall stile. Cross two fields then bear right to a stile by the river, a signpost points back to the bridge. The path you now follow is mostly by the riverside and is usually a dark green swathe across the grass. Shortly bear right when a path goes left away from the river. There are times when the path goes above the river but it returns to it. There is bird life about and after spotting a buzzard circling overhead, we saw a treecreeper searching a tree trunk, until it saw us. Look out for a stile in a wall a little to the left. From here the route reaches ancient **Ivelet Bridge**, a fine arched structure. There is a seat, in need of repair when prospecting the route. The bridge is associated with the old **Corpse Road**, when the dead were

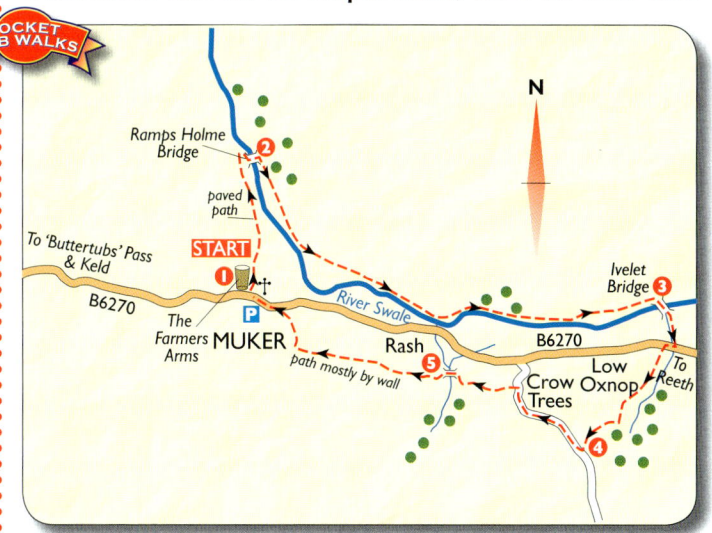

The Yorkshire Dales

Looking towards Gunnerside Pasture

carried from the upper valley for burial at Grinton. Traditionally the coffin was laid on the bridge while the mourners rested.

3 Cross the bridge and walk up to a road junction, with the stream running over the slabs. To the right is the old **Oxnop Bridge**. Cross the road to a wall stile on the right of the stream and go up the field in the direction signed. There is a steep climb up the side of a hill to a broken wall. Pass to the left of a large modern barn then go quite steeply down to a wall stile by a chicken run. Go right to a wooden stile and up a path, often muddy. Below and to the right is ancient **Oxnop Hall**. Cross a stony track and go straight up a grass bank. Bear a little left along the rim of the valley, with the stream below, to a stone stile near the end of a wall by trees. Continue a few yards to the wall corner. Go ahead a little and look for a gate in the wall, slightly left across the field.

The land is often wet and the path is not obvious on the ground. Reach the gate and turn right on the road.

4 Walk down for ¼ mile, with fine views emerging of the area. At a sharp bend reach **Crow Trees** on the right. On the opposite side of the road, go through a wall stile by metal gates. Go straight ahead on a hillside to a stile with a wooden gate. Some 100 yards in front there is a stile on the left in front of a barn. Turn right from it to a gap stile in a wall. Go down a few yards right to a wooden stile and descend by a wall. Keep by it over a small stream and up to a wooden stile. Go diagonally over a field, with a house on the right, to a small gate by the house entrance. Go left and down the track to a red gate. A footpath sign points over a bridge, with a plaque NWH 2007. Continue past **Rash View**, a signpost points straight on. At a second occupied property take care as you exit by black gates. Do not go ahead on the grassy track.

5 From the gates leave the track and drop down to a footpath on the right. Your route back to Muker mostly follows the wall by the sign. The path is awkward in places and you have to pick your way at times. There are compensations in the views which are revealed of the Swale and the rolling hills. When you reach an enclosed track go right and soon the familiar view of Muker is revealed, and you see the Farmers Arms.

Places of interest nearby

Hazel Brow Farm at Low Row, about 5 miles east of Muker, is an open farm where you can meet and feed the animals. At times there are demonstrations of farming methods and nature trails. Open Easter to end September. ☎ *01748 886224.*

Cartrake Force, is a spectacular waterfall near Keld, 3 miles north of Muker. It is a half-mile walk from Keld.

The Red Lion Inn

The valley of **Arkengarthdale** runs off Swaledale and is the most northerly dale in the National Park. There is wild country indeed beyond, but the walking around Langthwaite is something to savour. The first objective on this walk is to go to Booze! From there it is all downhill until you have three choices. The **long** walk has a climb up and down Fremington Edge, on a steep and slightly tricky descent. There is a **shorter** walk crossing Arkle Beck which involves some route finding, and is less easy than the **shortest** route, a level stroll to Langthwaite.

THE PUB

The **Red Lion Inn** has been featured in several films and TV series – cross the bridge to the Red Lion Inn and you may recognise it from the opening scenes of *All Creatures Great and*

Distance – 4, 3 or 2½ miles.

OS Explorer Outdoor Leisure OL30, Yorkshire Dales, Northern & Central areas. GR 005025.

Starting point The Red Lion Inn at Langthwaite.

How to get there Langthwaite is 3 miles north of Reeth which is on the B6270 through Swaledale. As you reach Langthwaite there is a village car park, and toilets further along the road.

Small. Look at the selection of real ales, including Black Sheep Bitter, Tetley's and Worthington's. You might fancy a Guinness or try a selection of the wines. There are bar snacks, and Cornish pasties and Melton Mowbray pork pies add a touch of the cosmopolitan! Hot drinks are available too. Books and maps are on sale and you will probably have a look at the many pictures of the TV stars who have been here.

Food is served from 11 am to 3 pm and 7 pm to 11 pm daily. In summer longer opening hours may be kept.
☎ *01748 884218.*

1 From the bridge walk through the small square with the **Red Lion** on your left and up the steep and narrow street between cottages. Keep on the road, ignoring turnings off. On the left are some narrow stone steps leading to a seat with a view. The road becomes unmade and the scattered houses and farms you reach are the hamlet of **Booze**. Though it is clearly marked on the OS map there is no sign 'on the ground', perhaps it would be too popular? Keep by the wall and go right at **Town Farm** on a paved path of sorts and through two gates to a footpath sign pointing down the field.

The Yorkshire Dales

2 Follow the sign down the field, through a wall gap and right at a sign along a grass track. Take the bridlepath signed to **Fremington**, by a green metal gate, down the track to reach a footbridge over **Slei Gill**. Keep on the track in front of houses to a bridlepath sign indicating **Hurst** to the left.

3 *For both shorter routes:* Continue ahead on the track and reach a black gate, with farm buildings to the left. Walk on the field path to a gap in the wall and continue in the second field to the river. Nearby a footbridge crosses **Arkle Beck**.

For the shortest route: Turn right and follow the instructions from Point 6.

For the shorter route: Cross the bridge and turn left following a walled track. Turn a corner and go up to a gate at **West Raw Croft Farm**. In the farmyard turn right onto a wide track

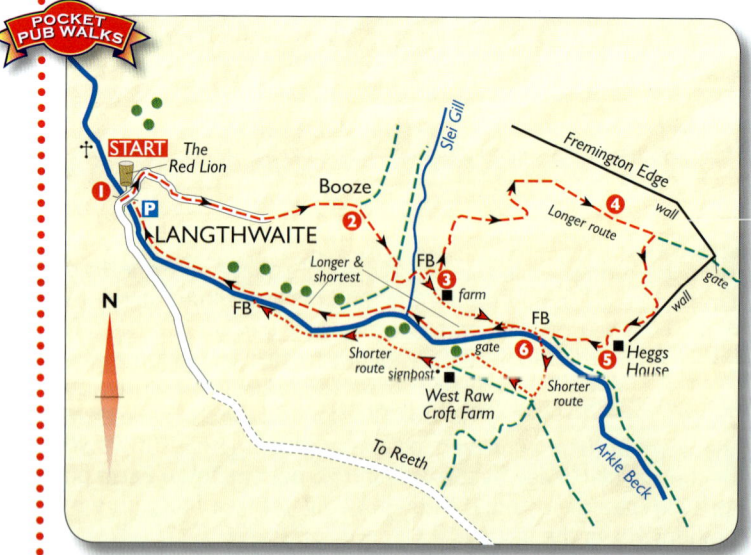

briefly then bear right on a narrow grass path. Reach a red metal gate by the wall, with a yellow waymark. Continue by the wall through a gap to a second gate. From here the path leaves the wall and goes half left up the hill. Head towards an electricity pole where a footpath sign nearby points back. Go ahead to a stile. The following stiles are mostly clear to find and the path is continuous. However, the ground may be wet and walking is not always easy. When you reach the riverside a path leads to a footbridge and you cross **Arkle Beck** again. Turn left on a clear track which leads you back to **Langthwaite**.

A shady path near Langthwaite

For the longer route: Turn as for **Hurst** and climb the sunken path which leads up the end of **Fremington Edge**. There is a zigzag at first, but keeping mostly near the wall on the left you then reach a gate in the wall above. Here you join Open Access land, and walk on tracks through an area of old mining remains. Turn right on a bridleway track marked **Hurst**, with yellow topped posts. At first you go back in direction but soon you are heading across open land with widespread views. There is grass to walk on and big cairns mark the way. On the right, off the path, you will see the large cairn which is a great viewpoint over **Arkengarthdale**.

The Yorkshire Dales

4 Return to the path and continue ahead, but soon you need a track down to the right. Shown as a green right-of-way on the OS map, this starts about 50 yards after a stone cairn and before the next one, well before the wall and gate ahead. The path is not signed but there is a walked line through the grass. It descends a little; then look for a turning left along a green track. Reach a wall ahead, which runs down from the top of **Fremington Edge** to the bottom. You will see your objective, the building below, **Heggs House**. The path leaves the wall and zigzags down through bracken and eventually reaches the house. You may see two signs pointing back up the hill indicating paths.

5 From the gate, go through the grounds of **Heggs House** which was unused at the time of writing. The track reaches **Arkle Beck** and from a gate you arrive at a footbridge.

6 Do not cross the bridge, but continue ahead beside the beck to a footbridge over Slei Gill. Go ahead, ignore a small gate on the left and pass through a tunnel. Ignore a footbridge over the river. At a signpost for **Langthwaite**, leave the river and soon you will see buildings ahead. Keep on the track and return to the village and the **Red Lion**.

Places of interest nearby

At Reeth the **Swaledale Museum** has a good display of the history of the area, particularly the lead mining.
☎ *01748 884118*

Richmond has the oldest stone-built Norman castle in the country and in the town the Richmondshire Museum has the surgery set from *All Creatures Great and Small*.
☎ *01748 825611*

8 **Redmire**

The Bolton Arms

This walk is a figure of eight. With the attractive Wensleydale village of Redmire in the centre you first go to Castle Bolton, forever associated with Mary, Queen of Scots, who was imprisoned here. The panorama you see from the castle is wonderful; it is one of the reasons we like to go walking. Completing the figure of eight you can take a ramble to the River Ure and a lovely riverside path to Redmire Force. You could do this route as one walk or two circular walks. Redmire featured in the popular TV series *All Creatures Great and Small*. In summer you may see a train on the Wensleydale railway, or even arrive by one!

'Walkers Welcome' says the board outside the **Bolton Arms** and it is as good a Dales pub as you will find. Walkers will appreciate its high standards, so you should take off those

The Yorkshire Dales

Distance – 5 miles.

OS Explorer Outdoor Leisure OL30, Yorkshire Dales, Northern & Central areas. GR 045912.

Starting point The Bolton Arms in Redmire.

How to get there Turn off the A684 at Wensley and follow the road for 4 miles. From Aysgarth it is about 5 miles to Redmire, travelling via Carperby.

boots before entering, as requested! There is plenty on the menu to tempt you, the home-made steak and kidney pie would be just the thing after a walk, and I was told that the curry dishes are always popular. The lunchtime menu includes sandwiches and baguettes, with vegetarian choices. John Smith's Cask and Black Sheep beers are here, with a guest beer just to make the choice harder! The comfortable rooms were patronised by some of the TV stars during the filming of *All Creatures Great and Small*.

Open all day Saturday; Sunday 12 noon till 5 pm and 7 pm till midnight; Tuesday to Friday 12 noon till 2.30 pm; Monday to Thursday 7 pm till midnight; Friday till 1.30 am. Restaurant open Tuesday to Sunday 12 noon till 2 pm and Monday to Saturday 7 pm till 9 pm.
☎ *01969 624336*

1. Start the figure of eight with the **Bolton Arms** behind you. Walk towards the village green and go left onto the main road. In a few yards, as the road bends, go right at a footpath sign. Follow this through stiles, ignore turnings right and go left, up a field edge. At the top corner find a stile and rejoin the road. Follow it under the railway bridge then turn left for **Redmire**

Station along the vehicle track. Reach the current terminus of the **Wensleydale Railway**. If you do *Walk 5* from Hardraw you see Appersett Viaduct, beyond Hawes, on the disused line.

2 Continue and, not far ahead, a footpath comes up from **Redmire** and crosses your track. Turn right to follow it, briefly, but when this track turns off right go ahead into trees. The narrow path emerges at a stile near a barn. Continue up the next field edge to a stile at the top corner. Go up a banking to a track running from right to left. It is surfaced in places and is shown as a yellow road on the OS map. Turn left on it and reach a gate.

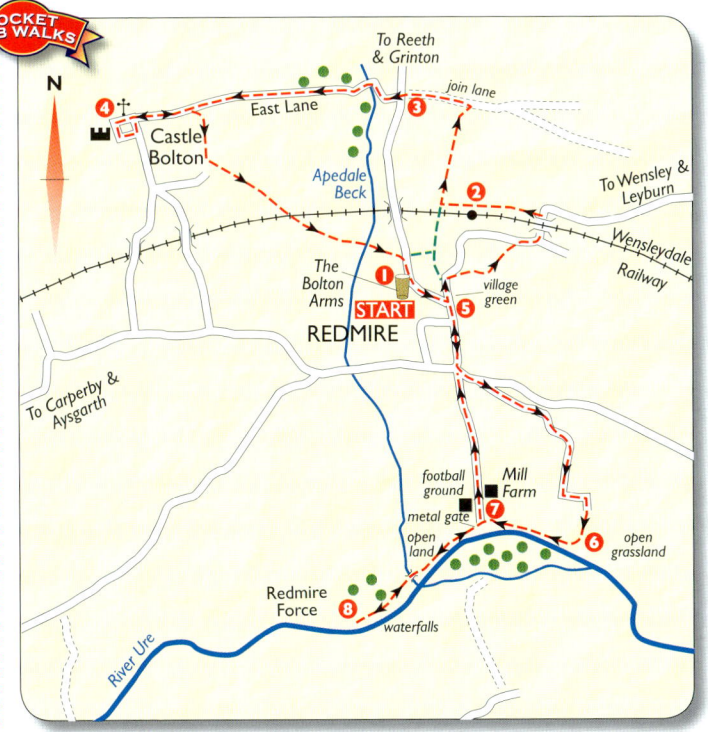

3 Cross the road and go towards **Castle Bolton**. This is **East Lane** which first crosses **Apedale Beck** where the stream bed is wide and rocky. In the thick hedge you should see plants in every season, with blackberries in autumn and red campion about. As you enter the village a remarkable

Castle Bolton

sight greets you – the wide grassy street is dominated by the towering castle, a view unique in the Dales. The castle is open daily from March to November. The gardens have a fine maze and a vineyard. There are toilets in the car park.

4 Continue the top of the figure of eight by retracing your steps down the main street. Towards the end of the houses on the right, bear right after **Penhill View** and take a footpath signed **Redmire**. From a gap stile go down to a crossroads of paths and left towards Redmire. Follow the grassy path over fields to the railway track. Cross it diagonally to a stepover and continue to a gap stile in the wall ahead. Follow by the wall to the footbridge across **Apedale Beck**. From a gap stile on the right go to a wall stile ahead. Cross half left past a wall corner to a wooden stile and a road. A right turn brings you to the **Bolton Arms**.

5 The bottom of the '8' starts with the **Bolton Arms** behind. Walk towards the village green and turn right at the fork. Go down the street to a bend in the road and left on the track signed to **St Mary's church**. In a few yards leave this lane and bear right at a footpath sign. Now follow an enclosed track, round several bends. Two fords are crossed, and at the next bend ignore a footpath going ahead and keep on the enclosed track. After two more bends follow a straight section to a metal gate. There is an open area of grassland, with the **River Ure** ahead.

6 Turn right by the wall and follow a fine, high-level path where the views down to the river are spectacular. The path is narrow, winding through rough ground. Reach a stile where you cross the bottom of a lane over to a metal gate ahead.

7 Continue into an area of grassland and follow the path down to the river level. We saw dippers on the water, bobbing up and down on stones. Reach a peculiar metal bridge over **Apedale Beck** and enter a wood. This path is a nice contrast to the grassland. Soon you reach rocks and with a little scrambling you are at **Redmire Force**.

8 There are three sets of falls, similar to those at Aysgarth, though on a smaller scale. The right of way goes no further and it is necessary to retrace your steps to the metal gate by the lane at Point 7. From the gate turn left up the narrow lane, do not re-cross the stone stile. Pass the football field and continue up to the road again. Return to the **Bolton Arms** to complete the figure of eight.

Places of interest nearby

At Leyburn Business Park you can see the chocolates being made at **The Little Chocolate Shop**.
☎ *01969 625288.*

Nearby at **The Teapottery**, eccentric teapots are made, including some for the TV programme **Countdown**, and the production area can be viewed.
☎ *01937 588235.*

9 Carlton-in-Coverdale

The Foresters Arms

Coverdale runs between Upper Wharfedale and Wensleydale and though it is not easily reached from either end, you will enjoy Coverdale's slightly hidden nature. It is a lovely, tranquil valley. This route uses some pleasant field and riverside paths. Being off the beaten track, many of the footpaths are only lightly walked. To reach the hilltop settlement of Swineside there is a slightly complicated climb through stiles which need to be found on land which is often wet, but the views are good. West Scrafton is an attractive village from where you make your way across the river back to Carlton.

THE PUB

The **Foresters Arms** standing on the main street in Carlton was originally an inn serving the drovers making their way along Coverdale. Then, as now, it would have been a welcome sight. The menu offers a British cuisine, including

Distance – 6¼ miles.

OS Explorer Outdoor Leisure OL30, Yorkshire Dales, Northern & Central areas. GR 067847.

Starting point The Foresters Arms, Carlton. Parking at the village hall, (honesty box).

How to get there *From West Witton or Wensley take roads south towards Melmerby and follow signs to Carlton. From Middleham follow Forbidden Corner signs, continuing on to Carlton. From Kettlewell, it is 10 miles via Park Rash.*

items such as game in season and fallow deer steak, as well as bubble and squeak. A good choice of beers includes John Smith's Cask and Black Sheep Brewery and you might be there when there is a guest ale from Yorkshire Dales Brewery or even Wensleydale Brewery. Given its location, the comfortable rooms at the Foresters are popular.

Open Tuesday to Saturday 12 noon till 2 pm, Sunday 4 pm; Tuesday to Sunday 6.30 pm till 11 pm. Food is available till 1.45 pm, evenings till 8.30 pm, except Sunday. It is closed all day Monday and Tuesday lunchtime.
☎ *01969 640272*

1 Leaving the **Foresters Arms**, go right on the main street and in a few yards turn right through a gateway at a footpath signed **Goodmans Gill**. Ahead, cross a stile then follow a path to the left and go down to a stream. Cross a footbridge and turn left up to a signpost at a wooden gate, marked 'Please shut the gate'. Now in a field, follow the arrow half right on a path over which you can see people have walked. The views ahead are of **Dead**

Man's Hill and **Little Whernside**, the boundary of **Nidderdale**. Reach a metal gate and a footpath sign, then continue across the field to a squeeze stile. There is a second stile in the wall ahead and from here the wall is on the left. Find the next stile about 200 yards ahead in the wall, just before a gateway. In this field head diagonally to a small wooden gate hiding another squeeze stile near the corner of the wall. Follow the wall to a road.

POCKET PUB WALKS

To Wensley

The Foresters Arms

START

CARLTON-IN-COVERDALE

To Middleham

Goodmans Gill

Caygill Bridge

N

2

6 West Scrafton

FB

River Cover

Gammersgill

3

Swineside **5**

fence

damaged walls

signpost

stone bridge

Woods Gill

Scalrigg Gill

wall

fence

To Kettlewell via Park Rash

4

Hindlethwaite Hall

Horsehouse

2 Go left here and soon see a footpath on the right signed to **Gammersgill**, starting with a stile. Go on a short path to a gate and stile, then walk towards a line of trees and another stile. Cross a stream and continue up into the field where the **River Cover** makes a big loop and can be seen through the trees. From a wooden gate look for the next stile some distance away at the end of a long field. The ground is hummocky and uneven but the way forward is clear. Keep

West Scrafton, visited on the walk

on to a narrow footbridge over **Turn Beck**. An enclosed section is a contrast, with trees and you may find hazelnuts around. At the end turn right half right to a wall stile and a road.

3 Go left into the hamlet of **Gammersgill** and, after only a few yards, take a left turn, marked **Swineside**, though you do not go there yet. Go right almost immediately to a footpath gate. Cross the field to a small wooden stile in the fence ahead, by a red metal gate. Continue in the same direction to a stile in a wall corner next to the river. There is a ford across the river here. Follow the riverside path for ½ mile and a second path joins from **Gammersgill**. Keep by the river, the path is slightly complicated at first but it is signed. Pass a stone bridge and continue to a narrow wooden footbridge which you cross.

4 Go left to a step stile and on a short path to a wall stile. Your objective is **Swineside** at the top of the hill ahead. Leave the wall in the direction of the signpost. Cross rough land and a stream and reach a stile to the right of trees. Cross a stream and go over a gap in a wall. The path goes through young trees to a second gap. Keep going up, finding stiles on a path which is continuous, but the walking is not always easy. The land levels out at a signed

The Yorkshire Dales

stile in the wall running up the hill near a fence. Cross a muddy area, where a stream emerges, and along a single line path, over a field to a damaged wall. The stile is slightly left, then over the next field to a stile. The buildings at **Swineside** are ahead as you go through a gap in a fence and a wall. Bear right by a barn to a wall stile on the right of a gate. A sign points back to **Horse House** and you pass **Little Swineside**. Walk up the lane away from the houses and turn left over a cattle grid onto a road.

5 Walk on this quiet road with widespread views of **Coverdale** and the slopes leading to **Upper Nidderdale**, the rocky outcrop is **Great Roova Crags**. Pass a house with several large bird boxes on its wall. Continue down the lane and into **West Scrafton**. Reach a small green, with seats and a red telephone box.

6 Take the footpath, signed by the chapel, to **Carlton**. Bear right to a footbridge and up to a grassed area. Go through a gate, turning left down a field to a kissing gate. Descend to a sign for **Caygill Bridge**, then find two bridges. A path goes up with the stream on the left. Turn right through a gate and follow a wall, continuing ahead when it turns left. Access a red metal gate and turn left on a tree-lined track. Ignore stiles going off and reach the road in **Carlton**. Turn left to the **Foresters Arms**.

Places of interest nearby

The Forbidden Corner, 3 miles from Carlton, is an unusual attraction. Described as a recent folly, a unique labyrinth of tunnels, chambers, follies and surprises have been created in a four-acre walled garden. Pre-booking is required ☎ 01969 640638.

At **Middleham**, the 12th-century castle, which was the childhood home of Richard III, has one of the largest keeps in England.

10 **Bishopdale**

The Street Head Inn

Bishopdale is the link between Upper Wharfedale and Wensleydale, and at Newbiggin, at its northern end, the Street Head Inn has been looking after travellers since around 1730. This walk reveals widespread views, including Castle Bolton which is seen across Wensleydale, and you also have a glimpse of the neighbouring dale of Waldendale. You are walking mostly in open country on field paths, though the waterfalls known as the 'cauldron' at West Burton are in a wooded area. Most people are impressed by West Burton's remarkable main street if they are seeing it for the first time. Note that there is a smaller settlement also called Newbiggin a few miles away near Askrigg.

The Yorkshire Dales

Distance – 4 miles.

OS Explorer Outdoor Leisure OL30, Yorkshire Dales, Northern and Central areas. GR 998859.

Starting point The Street Head Inn at Newbiggin in Bishopdale.

How to get there *Take the B6160 south from West Burton and after 2 miles see the Street Head Inn on the right. From Buckden follow the B6160 north through Bishopdale for 7½ miles. The pub car park may be used by readers of this book intending to patronise the Street Head Inn. Please check before parking.*

THE PUB The **Street Head Inn** has a relaxed atmosphere with its open fires and a spacious interior. The beamed ceilings remind you of its history as one of the oldest coaching inns in the Dales. You can enjoy the pub's cask-conditioned ales in the cosy bar and the wide selection of beers includes Black Sheep, Theakston's and John Smith's. The pub has a good reputation for its food which is plentiful, whether you have a bar or restaurant meal. I found plenty of choice on the menus – meat, poultry and fish, as well as vegetarian options. Owners Nigel and Joanne pride themselves on their comfortable en suite bedrooms with panoramic views.

Open all day at weekends from 11.30 am. Monday to Friday 11.30 am to 3 pm and evenings from 6 pm. Food served 12 noon to 2 pm and 6 pm to 9 pm.
☎ *01969 663282*

1 From the **Street Head Inn** cross the road and go down the narrow lane opposite. Turn left at the end and go along

Newbiggin's village street. When the road forks, bear right and follow the sign to **West Burton**. **East Farm** is on the left and the track climbs a little and bears left. Just beyond a red metal gate on the right, reach a wall stile with a small gate where you leave the track.

2 From the stile climb half left up the field to a stile in the wall ahead between a gap and a water trough. Go up the next field to a gate and gap in a wall corner. Continue to a gap and reach a stile. Hopefully you will see **Castle Bolton** across the valley, visited on *Walk 8*. Go up a little to a stile and keep on the darker green path where people have walked. The next stile you may pass by as there is a gap you can go through. Ahead is a barn where a sign points to **West Burton**. A path also goes to Forelands which you may identify on the OS map as a wooded area. Follow the West Burton arrow to a gate ahead, under trees. The path descends slightly to a farm. Go through two red gates to reach a yard. Ahead is **West Burton**, but this is visited later.

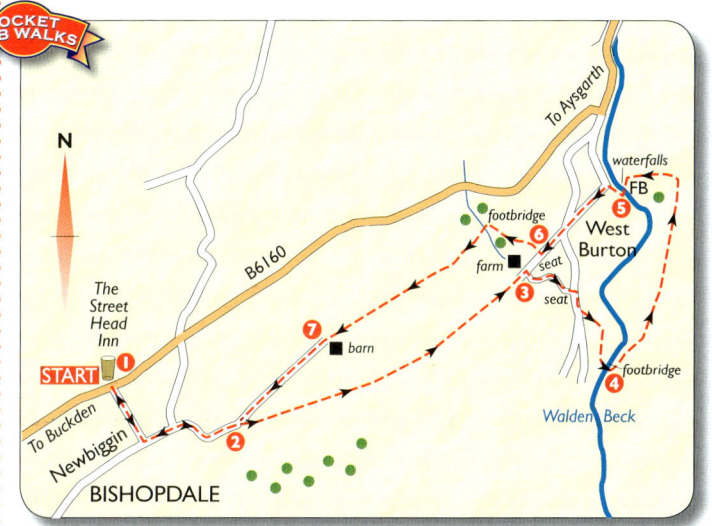

The Yorkshire Dales

The Cauldron Falls at West Burton

3 Turn right and go on the lane signposted to **Dame Lane**. After 200 yards reach a road and go right a few yards. On the left cross at a sign for **Cote Bridge**. Go down the field in the direction of the signpost arrow, to the right of the pylon, contouring above the stream. A second signpost points down to the footbridge over the stream. This is not **Cote Bridge** which is a little further upstream. The countryside seen ahead as you approached the bridge is **Waldendale**, a valley with no exit except on foot!

4 From the bridge go on the path signed to **Riddings**. The walking is relaxing on green paths, it is not necessary to identify every stile as they are easy to see ahead as you walk. The only habitation you see is **Riddings** which is above as you cross a field. Eventually the path curves down to a gate on the right. A yellow post marks the path and you cross a small stream. Follow the wall which turns to the left, and a sign for **West Burton**. Cross the stile and a narrow path brings you to a stone bridge

over **Walden Beck**. The spreading waterfall is **Cauldron Falls** and the stream once powered a woollen mill.

5 Continue from the bridge going between the houses and a left turn into the village reveals a fine prospect. This route includes the whole length of **West Burton** and its wide grassy greens. There is a shop on the right. Towards the top of the village, where a road forks left to Walden, keep straight on. Just after the first house on the right, about the end of the village greens, turn right along a footpath signed to the **B6160**. There is a seat across the road nearby.

6 Go on to the first stile to the left of a barn. At the bottom of the next field cross a stile in the corner of the wall ahead. Here you leave the B6160 path. Turn left and go over a stream. The path heads to **Newbiggin** and the next stile is clear. From a barn look along a wall on the left. Turn left to a stile by a wall and cross a field to a gap. Go over the next field to a stile, on the right of a metal gate. Cross the next field to a gate by a ruined building. Continue along the bottom of a field and reach a metal gate and the start of a green lane.

7 Follow the lane and reach the stile on the left from where you set out for West Burton. Go ahead, retracing your route back to the Street Head Inn.

Places of interest nearby

In Aysgarth, the owners of **Heather Cottage** have restored one of the few remaining Edwardian 'Backhouse' rock gardens in England. The gardens are opposite the cottage on the main road, at the end of the village going west. Admission is free.
☎ *01969 663229.*

11 Hubberholme

The George Inn

You are in a special part of the Yorkshire Dales at Hubberholme. Set in a quiet area of Upper Wharfedale, it is a good starting point for walks in classic limestone countryside. On this route, you climb at first, then a level section gives good views before a rocky descent to the hamlet of Yockenthwaite. The River Wharfe rises only a few miles up the valley and you follow it on a section of the Dales Way back to Hubberholme. The importance of this landscape is emphasised by the fact that large stretches are cared for by the National Trust. Several old traditions are kept up at the George Inn, which you may hear about.

Hubberholme Walk 11

Distance – 3 miles.

OS Explorer OL30, Yorkshire Dales, Northern & Central areas. GR 926782.

Starting point The George Inn at Hubberholme.

How to get there *Reach Hubberholme by the B6160, from Grassington to the south or Wensleydale to the north and turn at Buckden. There is parking on the roadside to the right of the church.*

The **George Inn** should feature in any book describing the pubs and inns of the Yorkshire Dales. Built as a farmhouse in the 17th century, the building remains largely unchanged with its thick stone walls and mullioned windows. Over time it has seen some sympathetic improvements and now it is a cosy, welcoming place and, so far, piped music and gaming machines have not reached it! The George serves generous portions of home-cooked food and the fish pie is popular in the afternoons. In the evening the chops are a speciality. There are usually Black Sheep and Skipton Brewery beers and a choice of over 20 malt whiskeys. In sunshine the south facing patio area is a fine place to be. If you want to stay, there are six en suite rooms available.

Open from 12 noon to 3 pm and 6 pm to 11 pm. Food served from noon to 2 pm and 6 pm to 8.30 pm. Closed on Mondays except bank holidays. Opening times may be reduced in winter and it is always worth telephoning first.
☎ *01756 760223.*

1 Cross the road from the **George Inn** and go over the bridge which spans the **River Wharfe**. Go right before the church and

left at the signpost up the track. The sign to **Yockenthwaite** is your route as the **Dales Way** soon turns off. Go up through a metal gate and, at a junction, follow the higher path to **Scar House** and **Cray**. There is a steady climb up a stony track which winds about, with a harder surface as it gets up towards a gate, with a stile to the right. Note the National Trust sign and continue up to **Scar House** which dates from 1698.

2 Go right behind the house and the track climbs up left, over limestone outcrops. At a signpost for **Cray** go left to a second signpost for **Yockenthwaite**. There is now more level walking. Follow the yellow posts, picking your way over rocky steps and soon a longer area of grass is reached. There are views down the valley through the trees. In spring, rock rose may be seen and thyme is about. Wrens are heard and there is certainly a chance of seeing a bird of prey in this area, circling overhead. Keep on towards woodland which you enter at a stile. The exit is over a footbridge crossing a deep gulley.

3 From the footbridge go down left to a gap stile with two gates. There is an old sheep pen on the left and ruins of other buildings indicate that this area has been occupied in the past. Keep along

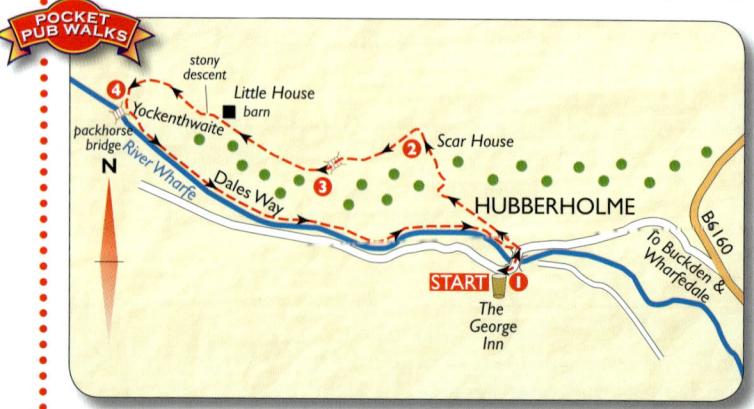

The stone bridge at Yockenthwaite

the escarpment through stiles and look out for a gap on the left which is the start of a footpath down the hillside. On the OS map this is below **Little House**, a stone barn standing at a higher level. Go down the path, which is clear but rocky in places, and may be slippery after wet weather. The path by the fence is easier; then reach a small gate and join a track. Go down and soon you are at the hamlet of **Yockenthwaite**. This was named by the Norse settlers and 'thwaite' means clearing, so this area was covered with trees in the distant past. The fine stone bridge was once on a packhorse route between Settle and Wensleydale.

The Yorkshire Dales

4 Here you turn left for **Hubberholme** on the **Dales Way**. See the signpost as you reach the farm buildings, and go across to a wooden gate on a track in front of the lower house. Cross over to a metal gate and then go right to a small gate and take the steps down to the riverside. From here the path is clear and generally well marked. It hardly leaves the river, and is a lovely stretch of countryside. The **Wharfe** rises about ten miles away at **Cam Houses**, where the same high land feeds the infant **River Ribble**. You may see trout in the river. Keep on towards **Hubberholme** where the church tower is first glimpsed through the trees. Follow the churchyard round and across the river stands the white-painted **George Inn**.

Places of interest nearby

People come to **Hubberholme** from far and wide to see the 12th-century church which is noted for its medieval rood loft, one of only two in Yorkshire. Among other interesting features are the pews, choir stalls and chairs made by the celebrated Robert Thompson, whose trademark was a carved mouse.

About 4 miles beyond Kettlewell there is plenty to do at **Kilnsey Park**. You can fish at the trout farm, look for red squirrels, feed the animals, go pony trekking – and see the Goat Skyway! Water flowing through the grounds also produces the Park's electricity needs and visitors can see the operation.

☎ *01756 752150.*

12 **Hebden**

The Clarendon Hotel

Hebden, near Grassington, provides a starting point for a streamside walk which is splendid in itself, and it is interesting to see the remains of the lead mining which once flourished here. A walk into the small metropolis of Grassington provides a contrast, with a fine stretch of the River Wharfe completing a longer walk than most in this book. There is also a shorter alternative which you can take from Hebden Gill, which still provides wide views. It is the shorter walk which has a descent for which boots are best.

The spacious **Clarendon Hotel** is a real ale pub, where you may find Timothy Taylor's, Tetley's Cask and Black Sheep beers, as well as guest ales. There is a good choice of food,

The Yorkshire Dales

Distance – 6¼ miles or 3 miles.

OS Explorer Outdoor Leisure OL2, Yorkshire Dales, Southern & Western areas. GR 025632.

Starting point The Clarendon Hotel at Hebden.

How to get there Take the B6265 Pateley Bridge road from Grassington and after 2 miles the Clarendon is on the left. On-street parking is available close by.

including pork loin and bangers and mash. At lunchtime there are specials and the Clarendon's sandwiches are always popular. Game in season is a highlight here. You will see pheasants on your travels in the Dales and the Clarendon might be the place to try a brace. Comfortable B&B accommodation is also available.

The Clarendon Hotel is open all day, every day. Food is served from 11.30 am to 2 pm Monday to Saturday and all day Sunday. Dinner is from 6 pm to 9 pm and booking is advisable.
☎ *01756 752446*

1 From the **Clarendon** turn left and take the first lane left, before the bridge. The stone cottages and trees make a fine picture as you walk away up the track, with **Hebden Beck** on your right. After the **Yarnbury** sign a post points right for **Thorpe Edge**, this is the return on the *shorter walk*. Keep on the lane to a collection of properties called **Hole Bottom**. From the wooden gate on the right, signed to Yarnbury, cross a stone bridge. Follow the beck on a track now unsurfaced. As you get higher the valley opens out and there are buildings ahead and remains of mining activity all around. After a gate, where the track divides, follow the lower, left-hand track by the water. Soon cross the stepping stones and go right to a gate. There is a fence across the beck and below it a ford.

2 *For the shorter walk to Thorpe Edge:* Go back and cross the stepping stones. Climb the banking ahead and go left on a path; a dry reservoir is below on your right. Bear right into the small valley and turn right on the gravel path which climbs to a higher level and through fields. Reach a gate and continue on a green path through more gates. From a gate with a signpost by a deep

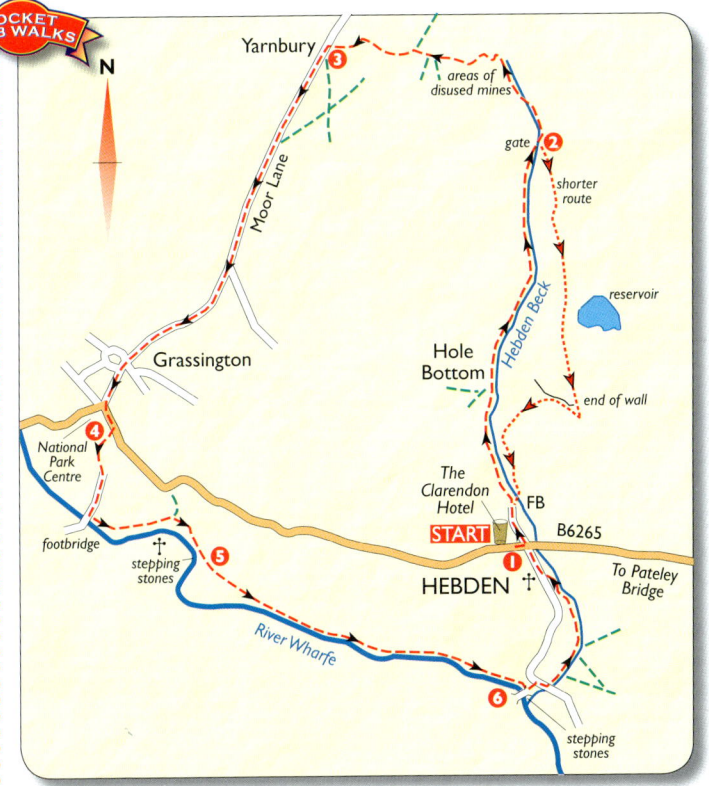

The Yorkshire Dales

The River Wharfe, near Grassington

gill follow a wall to the next gate. From the gate continue until the wall finishes. Here a vehicle track emerges from a property, follow this ahead for about 200 yards to a yellow post. Now leave the track and turn very sharp right, crossing a small moorland area on a narrow path to a wall stile with a signpost. Cross the stile and pass the entrance gate, walking by the boundary wall to a gap and a footpath sign. A path goes down, take care on the descent but the path is well used. Reach a small gate in a wall below. Go ahead on the grass, gradually bearing left to join the wall on the left as it curves round. You will see **Hebden** in sight as you walk down, crossing stiles to reach a footbridge. Regain the track and turn left to return to the **Clarendon Hotel**.

To continue the longer route: From the gate continue up the valley. The path crosses then recrosses the beck, then climbs to a stony area. It then goes left, with a zigzag, and soon reaches a gate with a bridleway signed right. Cross an open area with mining detritus and after a wide gap in a wall join a track and turn left. There is now a wide, smooth path to **Yarnbury**.

3 Turn left and follow the road down into **Grassington**. Walk through the town and leave the main street by a left turn onto the main road. Go along to the zebra and cross to the **National Park Centre**. There are toilets here.

4 Continue down to the left through the overspill parking and on to a narrow track signed to **Linton Falls**. Before the footbridge, cross the wall stile on the left, signed **Dales Way** to **Hebden** and **Burnsall**. Follow this easy path over the field. It becomes gravelled and goes up to a lane. Turn right and pass a fishery, then continue to a gate with a four-way signpost.

5 Follow the Burnsall direction and enjoy a lovely stretch of riverside walking, reaching **Hebden suspension bridge**, (built in 1885 by the local blacksmith). There are more stepping stones, and a seat.

6 Continue as though walking off the bridge and go on a short track to a stile. Go up the field to a road and turn right on it for a few yards. Immediately after a road bridge, turn left on a path signed **Hebden** and **Bank Top**. Go through an entrance gate and between two houses and gardens. The path is clear through gates and you continue at a Hebden sign. Cross a white stony track and go left of a wall. Keep on the clear path which winds through a valley and soon climbs up to the village street in Hebden. A right turn brings you to the **Clarendon**.

Places of interest nearby

Stump Cross Caverns, 5 miles east on the B6265, feature caves and unusual rock formations enhanced by spectacular lighting. There is a good shop and visitor facilities. Open daily March to end November, weekends in winter and school holidays. ☎ *01756 752780*.

Parcevall Hall Gardens has 16 acres of formal and woodland gardens and many Asian plants. Situated at Skyreholme about 5 miles east of Hebden off the B6265. Open April to October. ☎ *01756 720311*.

13 Embsay

The Elm Tree Inn

From the peaceful village of Embsay, near Skipton, you can take a route which encapsulates a typical ramble in the Dales, with moorland tracks, a rocky climb and widespread views. Embsay was once a centre of the textile industry and you see remains of small mills and factories around. A railway also came, and went, and after it closed enthusiasts revived and extended the line. The sound of trains and the sight of steam may be heard and seen as you walk. Embsay has a reservoir, and it has a crag, and fine views of the reservoir are seen from the crag – when you have climbed a steep path. Please note that this walk is unsuitable for dogs, which are not allowed on the Bolton Abbey Estate access area.

Distance – 3½ miles.

OS Explorer Outdoor Leisure OL2, Yorkshire Dales, Southern & Western areas. GR 009538.

Starting point The Elm Tree Inn at Embsay.

How to get there Embsay is 1 mile north of Skipton, across the A59. Follow the railway signs. If approaching from the west the Elm Tree Inn is about ½ mile further on at the top of the village. The village car park is adjacent to the pub.

THE PUB The **Elm Tree Inn** is a real ale pub and the choices can vary but expect to find Goose Eye's No-Eye Deer or Charles Wells' Bombardier. There is likely to be a guest beer or you could try a real cider, perhaps Weston's Old Rosie. With a tempting range of food, the lunch menu includes steak and ale pie or bangers and mash. Evening time offers grills such as Yorkshire gammon or BBQ chicken. Fish dishes are available on both menus. There are choices for children and you can eat outside at the front watching the world going by.

The pub is open Monday to Saturday from 11.30 am to 3 pm and 5.30 pm to 11 pm; Sunday 12 noon to 3 pm and 7 pm to 10.30 pm. Food is served from 12 noon to 2 pm every day; Monday to Thursday 6 pm to 8 pm, (Closed January to March). Wednesday and Thursday 6 pm to 9 pm. Friday and Saturday 5.30 pm to 9 pm, Sunday 5.30 pm to 7.30 pm. During the summer, the pub is open all day at weekends from 12 noon to 11 pm.
☎ *01756 790717*

[1] From the **Elm Tree Inn**, go right on **Pasture Road**. Pass **West Lane** and the new housing on the left. After Manor Farm on

your right, **Embsay Crag** comes clearly into view. The road goes right and you walk up, passing a lane forking left. The long wall ahead is the reservoir embankment. Pass **Crown Spindle Mill**, a reminder of the area's industrial past. At a Yorkshire Water sign you have reached **Embsay Reservoir**.

2 Go left and the road becomes unsurfaced and you see boats belonging to Craven Sailing Club. Keep on the walled track and there are fine views as you gain height. Go right at the junction and over a stile onto a path which is often wet. You have reached the **Bolton Abbey Access Area** and dogs are prohibited. Take the path with the high ground ahead and to your left. Blue-topped posts mark the way. At a signpost, go right towards the reservoir to cross a footbridge over a stream. From here the climb

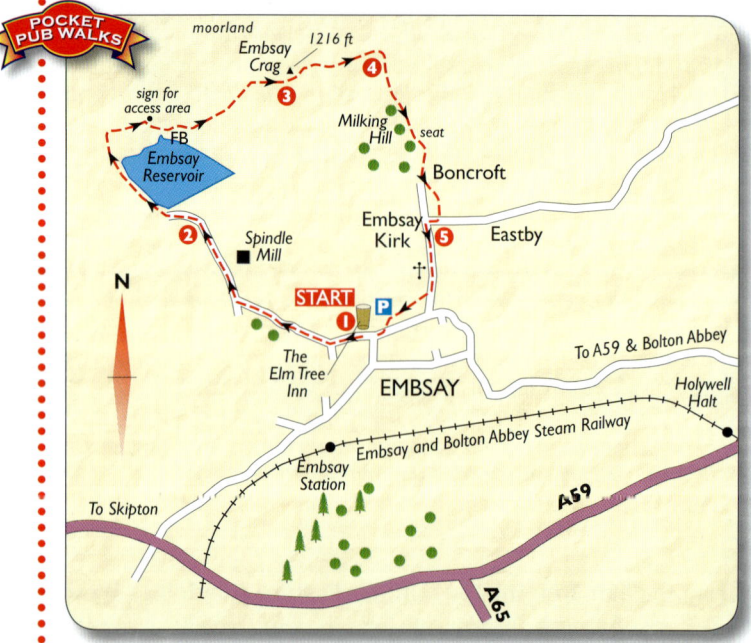

The reservoir seen from Embsay Crag

is through bracken with blue posts marking the way. Ignore a path going off left and contouring round the hillside. The path is quite steep and, at times, rocky. There are some diversions about but make sure you continue climbing. The 1,216 ft high top is a pleasant spot, with views to savour. When the heather is out in August and September the moors are a fine sight. Grouse are often heard calling at any time and you may see moorland birds flitting about.

3 Leave the top by a path on the opposite side. Like the path you came up on it is clear. You walk over a lower crag and look for blue top poles. The bracken is invasive and your path winds down to the right and goes parallel with the wall. This area is often muddy as water running down the hill does not escape easily. Look for a narrow sheepfold built against the wall and a few yards ahead reach a gate with a signpost.

4 Now head towards **Eastby** down a field on a green track. There is a stream on your right which you cross, then continue nearer the wall. Look across to see **Embsay Crag** in profile as you head down towards trees. Reach a gate and the track becomes enclosed by walls. The wall on the right soon ends and your interest might be taken by the valley on the right where trees are growing. Go down to a seat where a notice-board explains the area, known as **Milking Hill**. This wood is an asset to the Dales which is short of woodland and there seem to be many birds about. Continue down to **Boncroft Farm**, a 4x4 vehicle centre, and down the farm track. Follow this between fields to a road.

5 Turn right and keep on the road, passing **Embsay Kirk**. This is private but is significant as the first site of the original Augustinian priory, which was later rebuilt by the Wharfe and became Bolton Priory. Some 50 yards beyond **St Mary's church**, at the entrance to **Greenside**, go through a stile on the corner and follow the path diagonally over the field to the far corner. There is a short enclosed path and you access the car park by a stile.

Places of interest nearby

Steam trains run from **Embsay to Bolton Abbey station** each Sunday throughout the year, every weekend from April to October and every day from mid July to the end of August. Visits by Thomas and other special events also take place. ☎ *01756 710614.*

Hesketh Farm Park near Bolton Abbey village is a modern working beef and sheep farm open to the public as a 'hands on' experience. Visitors are able to feed some of the animals. Open Tuesday to Saturday from Easter to the end of the summer holidays, weekends from early September to October half term. ☎ *01756 710444.*

14 **Kirkby Malham**

The Victoria Inn

Malhamdale is renowned for its limestone landscapes. Most visitors head for Malham, the main village, but only a mile or so south the quiet village of Kirkby Malham is a good place from which to explore the area. Gordale Scar is probably the single most spectacular location in the Yorkshire Dales, and Janet's Foss is also a popular sight. These can both be seen on the longer of two walks and the surprising source of the River Aire is seen on both routes. On the longer walk there is a fair climb up to Weets Top, but the reward is the fine view enjoyed from its summit at 1,553 ft.

THE PUB

The **Victoria Inn** stands on the lane leading to the church in Kirkby Malham. It dates from 1840, just three years after Queen Victoria's accession. Steaks range from rump, sirloin and fillet to rib-eye, and landlord Granville also specialises in fish and

The Yorkshire Dales

chips, with mushy peas, of course! In summer you may find the Victoria serving food at midweek lunchtimes. The popular Tetley's and Taylor's beers are always on tap and there are guest ales. Open fires are a welcome feature and accommodation is available.

Food available Friday, Saturday and Sunday noon to 2 pm and 6 pm to 9 pm, Sunday 8 pm. Tuesday to Thursday 7 pm to 9 pm. No food on Monday.
☎ *01729 830499.*

1 Turn left out of the **Victoria Inn** and cross the main road. Follow the quiet lane past some interesting cottages and away from the village. As the lane bends left, there is a seat and you meet the **River Aire** and cross the bridge. The river has only come to the surface about one mile upstream, so this is the first of many bridges over a river that eventually flows under the railway station in Leeds, and on through industrial Yorkshire. Salmon have been seen in the lower reaches of the Aire. Here you join the **Pennine Way**, see the acorn symbol at the bridge stile. Go up the road, the impressive Hanlith Hall is on the right, and climb through the hamlet of **Hanlith**. At a sharp bend see a Pennine Way sign pointing left to **Malham**.

2 *For the shorter route:* Take this path and follow it up and down through gates and stiles. There are fine views, including Malham Cove ahead. After a footbridge over Gordale Beck, reach a pair of wooden kissing gates. Continue at Point 6.

For the longer route: Walk up the road and at a house named **Top of Hanlith** you have reached the area of **Windy Pike**. The track becomes unsurfaced, with views of **Malham** and the surrounding hills, including **Malham Cove**. Keep on the track, passing a wooded area on the left. The track turns right and left and you reach a gate at **Hanlith Moor**.

3 A footpath leads to **The Weets** across the Open Access land. The direction you need is a fairly direct line to a gate in the top

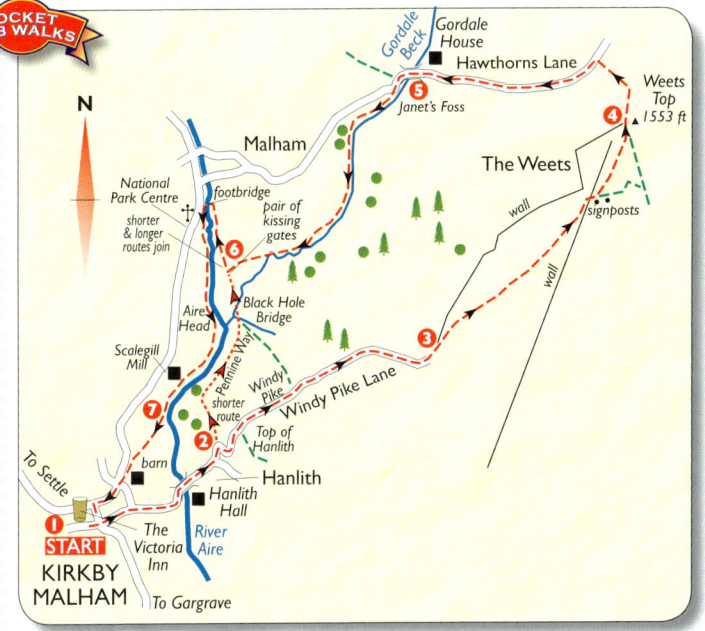

corner of the moor, where the long wall ahead meets a wall on the right along the top of the moor and which comes into sight as you go up. There are a few waymarks and the path is well walked. Sometimes it is necessary in wet places to divert from the line of the path. Reach the gate and, nearby, the first of two signposts points to **Weets Top**. About 200 yards ahead, join a firmer path which you follow to a gate and a trig point marking the summit.

The path to Gordale Scar.

4 Go through the gate and down the track signed to **Hawthorns Lane**, a quiet road where you turn left. Geologically you are walking through the Mid-Craven Fault and around you are limestone outcrops. Reach the optional turning for **Gordale Scar**, where an information board explains the 'extraordinary chasm'. You can take a level ¼ mile path to view the start of the rocky scramble.

5 Continue on the road over bridges to a footpath on the left signed as a riverside path to **Malham**. You first pass through **Janet's Foss** where **Gordale Beck** flows over a waterfall. Take care on the rocks which have become worn by many feet. Continue through and the walking becomes easier, a paved section is very pleasant. Reach a pair of wooden kissing gates at a T-junction of paths and turn right.

6 *Here the shorter route joins.* Follow the path and soon reach the outskirts of **Malham**. Cross a footbridge and from here you can look round the village. The **National Park Centre** is across

the road to the left, and there are toilets here. The route back to **Kirkby Malham** continues as a left turn from the footbridge. Go on the grass verge to a stile in the wall ahead, opposite the Methodist church, signed to **Hanlith Bridge**. From the stile cross the field to a gate near the right-hand wall. Cross a small footbridge and a gate just beyond. Keep ahead and up. The body of water emerging from the ground, and in the next field, is **Aire Head**, the start of the **River Aire**. This water has come from Malham Tarn, going underground soon afterwards at Water Sinks. It is a different stream which flows out of the bottom of Malham Cove. Continue from **Aire Head** through stiles and the path goes beside a millpond. You walk by the side of the former mill (Scalegill on the OS map) and exit at a gate by a drive.

7 Leave the drive and follow a field path, climbing the grass slope to a stile in a wall ahead. Continue across the next field to a stile to the left of a lone tree. Over the next field you pass a wall corner and go towards a barn. There is a roadside stile in the corner, by a 'road narrows' sign. A turn left on the road brings you back to the **Victoria Inn**.

Place of interest nearby

The story behind the 'watery grave' in the **churchyard** is of a sea captain and his wife whose married life was strained by the long periods the husband was forced to spend away at sea. When the captain died his wife decided that since they had been parted by water for so much of their married life, then it would be the same in death. The grave was so designed that the husband was buried on one side of a stream which ran through it. In time, the wife's wish to lie on the other side was denied when the gravediggers discovered rock which was too hard to penetrate. She was therefore buried above her husband.

15 Helwith Bridge

The Helwith Bridge

Ribblesdale is central to the Dales and contains its most celebrated hills – the summits of Whernside, Ingleborough and Penyghent. Known as Yorkshire's 'Three Peaks', they can all be completed in a 21-mile route. All three hills are seen, with long-distance views of the dale as you climb away from Helwith Bridge. You will enjoy a fine descent to the valley bottom and the 'Tay Bridge' over the River Ribble. Snaking through Ribblesdale is the line of the famous Settle to Carlisle railway, a great engineering project which changed the face of the dale in the 1870s. Faced with closure 100 years later, it was saved in an epic battle. You return to Helwith Bridge between the river and the railway.

Helwith Bridge Walk 15

Distance – 4½ miles.

OS Explorer Outdoor Leisure OL2, Yorkshire Dales, Southern & Western areas. GR 811696.

Starting point The Helwith Bridge, 2 miles south of Horton-in-Ribblesdale.

How to get there Helwith Bridge is 5 miles north of Settle on the B6479. As the road turns sharp right, go left at the sign for the pub. Across the road is a large open area for parking.

THE PUB **The Helwith Bridge** is the nearest pub to the railway in this book, only the width of the Ribble separates it from the line. Trains are much in evidence and when a steam special is on the way, don't be surprised if the customers run outside to watch it. The pub was built as a canteen for local quarry workers in about 1820 and, when the railway came in 1869, it became a hostelry for the 'navvies' working on the line. You may be rubbing shoulders with cavers, cyclists and campers. There is plenty of choice on the menu: the home-made steak and ale pie is always popular or you might try the Lamb Henry. Giant Yorkshire puddings are a feature with either Cumberland sausage or chilli. The variety of real ales will please you – up to eight available – plus local ale Three Peaks (brewed in Settle).

Food is served from 12 noon to 7 pm on Sunday, 12 noon to 3 pm and 6 pm to 9 pm on Saturday, 6 pm to 9 pm on Thursday (Steak Night) and Friday. At other times pies, peas and chips may be available. The pub is open Monday to Thursday 2.30 pm to midnight and Friday to Sunday noon to midnight.
☎ *01729 860220*

77

The Yorkshire Dales

1 From the **Helwith Bridge** go over the river and the railway and reach the main road. Cross over slightly left and then go right on the lane signposted **Dale Head**. The first part of this lane is a section of the **Ribble Way**, a long-distance route from Lancashire to the source of the river. Note the symbol of this route which you follow later. Bear left at a junction where the **Ribble Way** goes off right. Keep on the **Dale Head** track and eventually reach a wooden gate across the track. (Notice the Ordnance Survey benchmark arrow on the stone gatepost). The bulky hill you see ahead is **Penyghent** but you will have better views later. Along with the fine scenery, the sight of the

POCKET PUB WALKS

To Ribblehead

Horton-in-Ribblesdale

narrow lane

3

Dub Cote

wall

sycamore tree

Tay Bridge

4

bunkhouse

look for Dub Cote sign

2

gate

River Ribble

B6479

gate

quarries

N

5

HELWITH BRIDGE

START

1

To Austwick & A65

The Helwith Bridge

To Settle

The River Ribble, with Penyghent in the background.

quarry workings may strike you. These quarries are important to this area, and to the nation. **Horton Quarry** produces about 600,000 tonnes of stone each year, which is used in many ways and which is vital to our way of life. After a second gate reach a signpost pointing to **Dub Cote**. Across the valley and above the quarry see the flat top of **Ingleborough**, with **Whernside** away to the right and **Horton-in-Ribblesdale** below. By now you may have seen a train passing through the dale.

2 Here leave the track and cross the broken wall to turn right, following a fine springy grass track going down the field. Reach a wooden stile in a wall corner. Keep down by the wall and then the path does a wide sweep left and right to a stile by a gate. Go down to **Dub Cote** bunkhouse and a T-junction. Turn right on the lane and follow it past a junction, then right on a narrow lane, and down to reach the main road.

The Yorkshire Dales

3 Cross over and continue on an enclosed track. Ignore a ladder stile on the right and go next right by the farm buildings. A stream runs across the track but there are stepping stones. Reach a footpath sign pointing left. Cross a section of a field to a ladder stile and go on a track until it turns towards buildings. Ahead is a footbridge from where you reach a lone sycamore tree. Across the field, head for a bridge over the **Ribble** which you reach at the right-hand gap. A bridge stood here for many years which used timber from Tayside and gave it the name **Tay Bridge**. This was washed away in floods in 1953. It was rebuilt in 1996 with the aid of soldiers of 52 Field Squadron, Royal Engineers, from Ripon. Many local companies donated materials.

4 From the bridge go left on a section of the **Ribble Way** to **Helwith Bridge** which gives good views of **Penyghent**. On the river you may see dippers and other birds about. Keep by the river and pass near an industrial area. When the river makes a wide loop to the left, follow the path going away from it, over fields and through stiles. Reach a narrow footbridge but do not cross it.

5 The route is marked and you go away from the river and under a railway bridge. Cross the road to a path running alongside and provided by the Tarmac quarry company to avoid the narrow road. Soon you see the buildings at **Helwith Bridge** and you cross the road to a footpath which brings you back to the pub.

Places of interest nearby

At Horton-in-Ribblesdale the **church of St Oswald** dates from around 1100, with many interesting facets. The **railway station** is excellent for views of Penyghent and has won awards for its gardens, which are maintained by enthusiasts. Collections arranged by the Helwith Bridge pub landlord help to keep up appearances.